Protecting Habitats

Wetlands in Danger

Andrew Campbell

W
FRANKLIN WATTS
LONDON • SYDNEY

Designer Rita Storey
Editor Constance Novis
Art Director Jonathan Hair
Editor-in-Chief John C. Miles
Picture Research Susan Mennell

© 2005 Franklin Watts

First published in 2005
by Franklin Watts
96 Leonard Street
London
EC2A 4XD

Franklin Watts Australia
45-51 Huntley Street
Alexandria
NSW 2015

ISBN 0 7496 5819 3

A CIP catalogue record for this book is
available from the British Library.

Printed in China

Picture Credits
Cover images: Ecoscene (background and
centre); Still Pictures/Ronald Seitre (bottom
right)

Ecoscene: pp. 1 (Wayne Lawler),
5 (Wayne Lawler), 8 (Wayne Lawler),
9 (Dennis Johnson), 12 (Erik Schaffer),
14 (Nick Hanna), 16 (John Liddiard),
19 (Anthony Cooper), 20 (Phillip Colla),
21 (Anthony Cooper), 23 (Kjell Sandved),
24 (Anthony Cooper), 26 (Sally Morgan),
27 (NASA)
Eye Ubiquitous: p.25 (Hutchison Collection)
Still Pictures: pp. 4 (Dylan Garcia),
7 (Patrick Bertrand), 10 (Martin Harvey),
11 (Harvey) 13 (Gaethlich/UNEP),
15 (Jim Wark), 17 (Matt Meadows),
18 (Robert Galbraith), 22 (Fateh Singh
Rathore)

*Every attempt has been made to clear copyright.
Should there be any inadvertent omission, please
apply to the publisher for rectification.*

Note to parents and teachers
Every effort has been made by the Publishers to ensure that the
websites in this book are suitable for children, that they are of the
highest educational value, and that they contain no
inappropriate or offensive material. However, because of the
nature of the Internet, it is impossible to guarantee that the
contents of these sites will not be altered. We strongly advise that
Internet access is supervised by a responsible adult.

CONTENTS

What are wetlands?

Wetlands are habitats that form a link between land and water. They may be covered in water all the time or only after flooding, and can be home to a wide variety of plants and animals. Swamps, marshes and floodplains are all types of wetland.

Wetlands are also some of the most endangered habitats on Earth. Scientists think that around half of the world's wetlands disappeared during the 20th century. Wetlands face many different threats, from drainage and dam-building to pollution and global warming. In this book you will find out about these threats, as well as what is being done to protect wetland habitats.

How are wetlands made?

Some wetlands occur where the land meets the sea; others exist inland. A coastal wetland forms when a river slows down as it approaches the sea, causing the sand and mud it carries to sink to the bottom. Over time, this sediment builds up into banks, on which plants grow. The plants then trap more sediment and allow wetland habitats, like salt marshes, tidal flats and, in tropical regions, mangrove swamps, to develop.

Inland wetlands include floodplains, freshwater marshes, swamps and peatlands. A floodplain is a seasonal wetland, created when a river bursts its banks and flows over a surrounding area. Freshwater marshes and swamps are waterlogged more

Wetlands around the world, such as this peat bog in Ireland, are under threat from human activity.

permanently than floodplains. A marsh tends to be home to smaller plants while trees often grow in swamps. Another type of wetland, peatland, develops where there is not enough oxygen in the soil to break down dead plants completely. Instead, the plants sink into the ground where they eventually build up into peat.

What are wetlands like?

Each type of wetland has its own sights, sounds and smells. In a steamy mangrove swamp the only sound might be the plop of a mangrove seed falling from a tree into the mud. A salt marsh might be similarly quiet during winter, with only the sound of wind rustling through the sea grasses. However, summer brings the arrival of thousands of wading shorebirds, which means there is plenty of noise and activity.

But there are similarities between wetlands, too. They are often smelly places, because their watery soils lack oxygen. As a result bacteria produce gases when they break down food. More importantly, wetlands are often wild places where few people go, and provide a refuge for rare animals. All over the world, wetlands support many different species of plants and animals, as well as millions of people.

These flamingoes are pictured at their only European breeding site, the wetlands of the Camargue in the south of France.

Wetland diversity

Wetlands cover around 6% of the Earth's surface. They occur in every type of landscape, from mountainsides to jungles, and from deserts to the frozen Arctic.

Big and small

Some wetlands are as small as a village pond, while others are vast and provide habitats for many different species of plants and animals. The Pantanal of southern Brazil and northern Paraguay, a floodplain that extends for nearly 645 km (400 miles) along the Paraguay River, is the largest wetland in the world. The Prairie Potholes of southern Canada and the northern United States also extend for a great distance, but are made up of thousands of tiny wetlands in the form of potholes that fill up with water from melted snow and ice in spring.

Hot and cold

Wetlands exist in some of the hottest and coldest places on Earth. Desert wetlands look like dried-up mud channels for much of the time, but after a rainstorm plants will burst into life, providing a temporary home for insects and other animals. The seeds of these desert wetland plants can survive years in dry ground, waiting for rain. Seeds of the sacred lotus plant, for example, can last for hundreds of years in dry soil before coming to life.

There are also wetlands in the Arctic regions of Siberia, Greenland and northern Canada. These wetlands are a type of peatland known as tundra. For most of the year, apart from a few months each summer, tundra remains frozen solid. The summer sun melts the ice on the surface of the tundra, although only a few centimetres

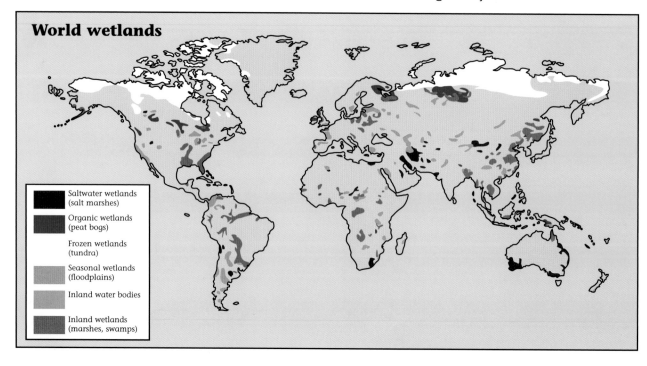

World wetlands

- Saltwater wetlands (salt marshes)
- Organic wetlands (peat bogs)
- Frozen wetlands (tundra)
- Seasonal wetlands (floodplains)
- Inland water bodies
- Inland wetlands (marshes, swamps)

underneath the ground remains frozen solid. The melted water has nowhere to drain away, and so forms pools and bogs where plants rapidly grow. In turn, these plants attract insects and animals, some of whom migrate (travel long distances) to feed and mate on the tundra.

Artificial wetlands

Farmers in China and southeast Asia create artificial wetlands, called paddies, in which to grow rice. The farmers usually build these paddies near coastal wetlands or floodplains and wait for them to fill up with water. They prevent the water from draining away by constructing low banks around the paddies.

Farmers do not plant rice seeds in the waterlogged paddies, but transfer the plants when they are still quite young. After it has become fully grown the rice is ready to be harvested. In countries such as Vietnam, Indonesia and China, many people still do this job by hand.

Wetlands occur in both hot and cold climates. This aerial view shows a bog in northern Finland.

Wetland plants

Nearly one-third of all plant species live in wetland habitats. One big difference between these habitats and other places, such as forests or oceans, is that they are often unstable. Plants may have to cope with wet and dry seasons, or with saltwater and freshwater.

Floating plants

Floating plants grow on the watery surface of wetlands. Some floating plants, like duckweed, float across the water while others, like water lilies, have roots in the mud underneath. Floating plants are well adapted to wetland conditions. The roots of water lilies, for instance, have special air-filled tissues that allow them to store oxygen. Some floating plants can adapt too well, however. The water hyacinth is a native species of South America, but in the 19th century plant collectors introduced it to other parts of the world. Today, it has spread out of control in parts of North America, Africa and Asia. Despite this, it can serve useful purposes: people use it as a cattle feed and as a natural fertilizer.

Carnivorous plants

Carnivorous plants are found in boggy wetlands where the soil has few nutrients. To make up for this missing source of energy, these plants kill and digest insects and even small animals. One famous carnivorous plant is the venus flytrap. Another is the pitcher plant, which grows in North America

Trees in swampy coastal areas often have stilt-like roots. These spider mangrove trees grow in a coastal area of Queensland, Australia.

REEDS, BULRUSHES AND SEDGES

Reeds, bulrushes and sedges grow in wetlands all over the world, from tropical swamps to Arctic tundra. They are known as emergent plants because their roots grow in the soil under the water, while their stems stick out (or, emerge) above the water. Humans have found uses for these plants for thousands of years. The ancient Egyptians used papyrus, a type of sedge, to make paper. People have traditionally used rushes for weaving baskets and making flooring and used reeds for thatching the roofs of houses. Today, reeds have another use: treating sewage. The stems of reeds act as filters, trapping large particles of sewage, and the micro-organisms in their roots eat away at toxic material in the sewage, breaking it down into harmless chemicals. Natural sewage treatment centres using reeds are much cheaper to maintain than industrial treatment sites. Since the 1990s the number of reed-bed treatment centres has grown in countries such as Germany, Australia and India.

and southeast Asia. It gives off a sweet-smelling nectar, which lures insects, lizards and frogs into its cup-shaped leaves. Once inside, the victim slips down the walls of the leaves and drowns in the rainwater that collects at the bottom.

Sphagnum moss

Sphagnum moss grows in even boggier conditions than carnivorous plants, where the only source of water is from the rainfall. Unlike other wetlands, which are also fed by rivers or underground springs, these bogs have very few nutrients indeed, and not very many plants can survive. Sphagnum moss, however, can absorb up to 15 times its weight in water. It is therefore able to extract the maximum goodness from rainfall, and can also stay moist even when there is no rain for a long time.

The sundew is a type of carnivorous plant that is common in boggy areas. It uses sticky hairs to trap insects, such as this cricket.

Wetland animals

Wetlands can be meeting points for many different animals, who are attracted to the water, the chance to hunt prey or eat lush plants and to mate. The Okavango Delta in Botswana, for instance, is a habitat for more than 600 species of birds, as well as hippos, snakes and big cats.

Animal adaptations

Like wetland plants, wetland animals have adapted to the specific conditions of their habitats. Lungfish, which are found in Africa, Australasia and South America, are a good example. These amazing fish can survive in or out of water. When the water level drops, the lungfish digs a burrow, covers itself in mucus to stop itself from drying out and starts to breathe air through a simple set of lungs. It stays in this burrow until the waters rise again, when it uses its gills once again to take in oxygen.

Amphibians and reptiles

Amphibians and reptiles are also adapted to life in and out of water. Amphibians, such as frogs, toads and newts, spend a lot of time on land but return to water to breed. Their offspring are tadpoles. These have gills for breathing water, which eventually turn into lungs for breathing air.

Snakes are one member of the reptile family that can flourish in wetlands. The grass snake of Europe and North America, for example, is an expert hunter both in and out of the water. The most famous wetland reptiles, however, are crocodiles and alligators, which live in tropical and semi-tropical wetland regions. They are particularly well suited to these habitats, having eyes and nostrils on the top of their heads so that they can move virtually hidden through the water in search of prey. Alligators in the Everglades marshlands in

The Okavango Delta in Botswana is a haven for wildlife such as these red lechwes, a type of antelope.

Scientists are keen to learn more about the migrating patterns of birds so they can ensure that their wetland destinations and stopping-off points are not under threat. One study that began in 2002 involves tracking light-bellied brent geese, which make the longest migration of any goose species. They journey from their winter home in Northern Ireland to their nesting sites on the Queen Elizabeth Islands in northern Canada. Using satellite technology, scientists have discovered that the birds stop off at Iceland and Greenland on the way. They hope that this information will help them maintain the population of this species.

Florida, in the USA, also have a way of coping with dry conditions. To survive, they dig "gator holes" in layers of soft rock that then fill up with water. The holes also attract fish and birds, and so provide the alligators with a source of both food and water.

Migrating birds

Coastal wetlands such as tidal flats and salt marshes are home to some of the world's biggest concentrations of birds. Most of these birds are migratory, which means that they breed in one wetland and fly elsewhere when the season changes, usually stopping off at other wetlands during their journeys. Each year, up to 12 million birds visit the Wadden Sea, a huge coastal wetland that stretches from Denmark to the Netherlands. The birds include lapwings, plovers, sandpipers and snipe, all of whom breed in the Arctic tundra during the summer months and spend the winter along the Wadden Sea.

The mudskipper is a type of fish that lives in tropical mangrove swamps. It has specially adapted fins and gills to help it survive out of water for long periods of time.

Wetlands and people

Workers plant rice seedlings in a flooded paddy field in northern Malaysia.

The relationship between people and wetlands stretches back over 10,000 years, when people in the Middle East first began to farm on the floodplains of the Tigris and Euphrates rivers. Today, wetlands continue to provide people with food and water, as well as protection against storms and floods.

Storing and cleaning water

Wetlands act like enormous sponges, soaking up water and drawing it down into underground aquifers (layers of rock that contain water). Aquifers, together with lakes and rivers, store large amounts of the world's freshwater. They are very important sources of water since most of the Earth's freshwater is inaccessible, hidden deep underground or frozen at the north and south poles. The passage of water from wetland to aquifer also filters out particles of soil and waste, making the water cleaner.

Wetlands, therefore, have a massively important role in providing people with water. This role grows more essential every passing year given the increasing water shortages many people face. One out of every five people in the world today does not have access to safe drinking water. Scientists warn that this figure may have risen to two out of three people by 2025.

Calming floods and storms

Wetlands also protect homes and communities against floods and storms. Wetlands on higher ground soak up heavy rainfall, while floodplains on lower ground prevent floodwater from moving too rapidly over the land, damaging property and

People around the world continue to coexist with wetlands in the ways they have done for centuries. The inhabitants of Vientiane in Laos, southeast Asia, build their houses on stilts so that they can endure the annual flooding of the Mekong River. The people who live on the shores of Lake Titicaca in Peru make their homes – as well as boats, furniture and musical instruments – out of reeds. And the Shanabala people of Sudan live on the country's floodplains. A nomadic people, they follow the receding floodwaters from place to place with their herds of animals to ensure they graze the freshest pasture available.

threatening people's lives. Experts believe that one explanation for the devastating floods in Bangladesh in 2004 is irrigation systems, which drain water from rivers and wetlands, causing them to dry up and lose their ability to hold floodwater (see pages 14-15). Coastal wetlands also protect shorelines from storm damage. Wetland plants absorb the energy from surging waves.

Providing food

Wetlands are a major source of food. More than half the world's population depends on rice, which grows in flooded paddies. When floodplains dry out, after rainy seasons, they are very useful because they provide rich grazing pasture for cattle, sheep and goats. Farmers graze more than 2.5 million of these animals on the floodplains of the Niger Delta in Mali, West Africa. Wetlands are also places where huge numbers of fish and other aquatic animals are born and raised, including herring, salmon, carp, lobster and shrimp. Around two-thirds of all the fish we eat have depended on wetlands at some point in their lives.

People living around Lake Titicaca, in Peru, depend on the wetlands that surround the lake for their livelihoods.

Drying out

While some communities have lived in harmony with wetlands for many centuries, other people have tried to drain them dry. This is nothing new: the people of ancient Rome, for instance, drained large parts of Italy. Today, however, with modern machinery and the building of dams and irrigation systems to control river systems, wetlands are more threatened than ever before.

Why drain?

There are several reasons why people drain wetlands. One reason may be to combat diseases, such as malaria, which is spread by mosquitoes that breed in wetlands. People also drain wetlands to build roads, factories, towns and cities over them. London, New York and Mumbai were all built on coastal wetlands. But the most common reason why people drain wetlands is for agriculture. Drainage makes grazing land usable all year round, not just in dry seasons. Drainage also means that farmers can grow arable and vegetable crops, which would rot or die from lack of oxygen in wet conditions.

These reasons appear sensible, but the price people pay for drainage can be high. Not only does drainage destroy wetland habitats, it can also cause land to shrink as the soil dries out. This drier soil is more vulnerable to wind and rain erosion and can also become more acidic, affecting crops.

A dredger clears an area of mangrove wetland on the island of Grand Cayman, in the Caribbean, to make way for a housing development.

A view of Buffalo Creek Dam in Colorado, USA. The construction of huge dams can have a dramatic impact on wetlands both up- and downstream.

Damming and diverting

Dams and irrigation schemes take water away from rivers and stop it from reaching wetlands, causing the wetlands to dry out. As with drainage, there are usually good intentions behind these projects: dams provide hydroelectric power, a cheap form of electricity, while irrigation schemes provide farmers with a steady supply of water.

But such schemes can have devastating effects on wetlands, including the loss of rich floodwaters for floodplains and the loss of freshwater for coastal wetlands, which then die from too much saltwater.

One example of the effect of dams has been seen in the floodplains of the Yellow River Valley in northern China. Because dozens of dams draw water away from the river to irrigate cotton fields, for 200 days each year the river no longer makes it to the sea. As a result the floodplains and the coastal wetlands of the Yellow River have begun to dry up. This is becoming an increasing concern for the Chinese government.

Fragile habitats

Drying out is not the only threat that wetlands face. Pollution, the overuse of wetland resources and tourism can all create major problems.

Pollution

Wetlands can absorb a certain amount of pollutants, but too much sewage and too many chemicals can be harmful. Big factories and farms are responsible for a lot of wetland pollution. Pollutants such as toxic chemicals, which get into wetlands from rivers, the soil or the air, can poison wetland habitats and cause plants and animals to die. Another harmful effect comes from fertilizers, which farmers spread on their land to improve their soil (see pages 18-19).

But we all share some responsibility for the state of our wetlands. Household detergents, such as washing powders and washing-up liquid, can damage the water quality of these habitats. Wetland experts urge people to use less detergents and to buy cleaning products that are more environmentally friendly.

Overexploitation

Another problem for wetland habitats is overexploitation, which occurs when people use too many natural resources without replacing them. Examples of overexploitation include people destroying mangrove swamps by chopping down mangrove trees for fuel, or catching huge numbers of fish, causing fish-eating birds and other animals to starve.

A field of peat cut ready for collection. Peat bogs are under threat from overexploitation.

This area of wetland in the United States has been polluted by waste water from a mining operation.

The best-known example of wetland overexploitation, however, is the digging up of peat from bogs and fens. Peat builds up very slowly, but during the 20th century people began to use it in much greater quantities than it could replace itself. Some countries with large peatlands, such as Ireland and Finland, have developed peat-fired power stations. Gardeners spread peat on soil, as peat improves it by breaking down the clay. Environmental campaigners have worked hard to stop the overuse of peat but people continue to dig it up. In addition, peatland is also drained to make more room for grazing livestock.

Peatland is not just important as a habitat. It also acts as the Earth's lungs. When peatland plants die, instead of releasing carbon dioxide (CO_2) into the air the gas is trapped in the peat, which helps keep levels of CO_2 in the atmosphere down. On the other hand, when peatland is burned to make room to plant crops, it releases huge amounts of CO_2 into the atmosphere, which scientists believe adds to global warming.

Tourism

Wetlands are special places where people sail boats, fish, watch birds and enjoy nature. But tourism can cause problems. Tourists might trample on wetland plants and drop rubbish. New roads, campsites and hotels are built to attract even more tourists. The best solution is ecotourism. This involves teaching people to understand natural habitats so they harm them as little as possible. Ecotourism holidays have become popular in Kakadu National Park, a major wetland area in Australia's Northern Territory. The Australian government is working with the Aboriginal people of Kakadu – who have lived there for over 25,000 years – to promote ecotourism.

17

Plants in danger

Fertilizer damage: a researcher surveys an algae-covered lake in Canada.

Plants are often the first living things in wetlands to suffer from drainage, pollution or overexploitation.

Plants have a vital role in habitats as the basis of food chains. Watermeadows, for example, are grassy floodplains on which farmers graze their cattle and sheep. In the past, farmers would cut the grass in these meadows in late summer, which gave wildflowers enough time to grow and produce seeds. The wildflowers attracted butterflies, insects and dragonflies, which in turn attracted birds, small reptiles and mammals that fed on the insects. In the 20th century, farmers in Europe drained huge stretches of watermeadow and replaced them with single species of crops or grass. This wiped out entire food chains.

The problem with fertilizers

Fertilizers, which farmers use to improve the growing conditions in the soil, can run off fields and get into nearby rivers and wetlands. A big problem with fertilizers is that they can upset the natural balance of wetlands by adding nutrients to the water. These nutrients encourage certain plants to grow very well, forcing out other plants that may be a main source of food for animals. Algae is one plant that fertilizers encourage to grow, causing a green, scummy surface on rivers and wetlands. Algae can reduce the amount of oxygen in water, making it hard for other plants and fish to survive.

In the Florida Everglades, pollution from fertilizers has encouraged the growth of bulrushes. In turn, the bulrushes have killed off large areas of saw grass, a type of sedge. To deal with this problem, scientists have built filtration marshes between farmland and the Everglades to absorb the worst effects of the fertilizers.

FUTURE MEDICINES

One reason why it is so important to save wetland plants is that some may possess the power to cure diseases. Wetland plants have already made major contributions to medicine. The willow tree, for instance, grows alongside rivers and in peatland areas. Its bark is the source of the chemical used in aspirin, a drug that provides pain relief and helps people who have heart problems. Scientists at the Royal Botanic Gardens in Kew, London, are currently studying as many wetland and other plants as possible to see if they might contain compounds that could help treat diseases such as AIDS or malaria. The threats to wetlands and other habitats make their work all the more important – if these plants became extinct then we might lose potentially life-saving medicines forever.

Sustainable farming: workers on the Somerset levels, a wetland area in southwest England, harvest willow withies, which are used to make baskets, furniture and even eco-friendly coffins.

Animals in danger

Some of the rarest animals in the world live in wetlands. Damage to these habitats means that some species are struggling to survive. They include the bittern, which is a type of wading bird, the otter and the manatee, a large water mammal that lives in tropical and semi-tropical wetlands. Some wetland animals, such as species of frog and dragonfly, have already become extinct.

Birds in danger

Populations of migrating birds have been particularly affected by the destruction of wetlands. Drainage of the Florida Everglades caused the number of birds to fall from 1.5 million to around 50,000 during the 20th century. However, recent efforts to restore this habitat have meant that their numbers are rising again. Pollution, as well as drainage, can be very harmful to birds. Toxic chemicals can make birds lose weight, while females produce eggs with thinner shells. These shells then break more easily, which means that fewer young are born.

New species, new problems

Like plants, wetland animals are also at risk from the introduction of new species that

These West Indian manatees live in mangrove swamps around the Caribbean.

STOPPING POACHING

As in other wild habitats, poaching can be a major problem for rare animals. In the Pantanal in Brazil and Paraguay, poachers hunt caimans – a type of alligator – for their skins. Conservation groups have worked to educate local people about the risk of extinction that this animal faces. They have also encouraged people to set up commercial caiman farms. The farms do not harm the wild population and, in addition, they enable people to earn more money than they would have done through illegal poaching.

may force them out of their habitat. The introduction of the Nile perch to Lake Victoria in eastern Africa has led this fish to dominate the lake, taking away food from other species. Scientists fear that up to 60% of the species that lived in Lake Victoria may now have become extinct.

Protecting animals
Countries around the world have become more aware of the need to protect their endangered animals in wetlands. The governments of India and Bangladesh have made part of the Sundarbans, the world's biggest mangrove swamp, a tiger reserve. The Sundarbans is the last remaining habitat of the Bengal tiger, and the governments hope the reserve will ensure its survival. Similarly, part of the Okavango Delta in Botswana is now a wildlife reserve, to protect the rare bird and animal species that depend on it.

This view of a European coastal salt marsh shows a large flock of wading birds, including hundreds of gulls.

Protecting wetlands

The international campaign to save wetlands began in 1971, when 18 countries signed the Ramsar Convention on Wetlands of International Importance, in Ramsar, Iran. By 2004, 138 nations had signed this convention, promising to safeguard the major wetlands in their countries – a total of 1,368 wetlands around the world.

Lots of schemes

The Ramsar Convention has been joined by other international schemes to protect and care for wetlands. These include Agenda 21, produced by the United Nations at the Earth Summit in Rio de Janeiro, Brazil, in 1992. The United Nations called the summit, or meeting, to try to solve a number of environmental problems facing our planet, including endangered wetlands. Other schemes include efforts by the European Union and environmental organizations.

But do they work?

One good thing about international protection schemes is that they draw attention to endangered wetlands. For example, when the Mai Po Marshes in Hong Kong became a

Some endangered animals depend on local wetlands for survival. These tigers live in Ranthambore National Park in India.

This photograph shows scientists in a mangrove swamp in Panama collecting samples to help a wetlands research project.

listed site under the Ramsar Convention, more people became aware of the need to preserve this wetland, which is an important breeding ground for herons, pelicans and eagles. One frustrating thing about international schemes is that they are only agreements between countries, and not actual laws. Agreements cannot force people or governments to protect wetlands.

Sometimes individual countries can be better at protecting their wetlands. The Flow Country is an area of peatland in Scotland that is home to mosses, heather and bulrushes, as well as rabbits, deer and lots of different birds. When the planting of trees began to threaten this habitat, campaigners persuaded the government to make part of the peatland a protected site and ban tree-

planting. Many major wetlands cross national boundaries, however, so countries must co-operate with each other if they are to ensure the survival of these habitats.

What does protection mean?

There are two main ways of protecting wetlands. The first way is to encourage the owners of farms and factories to look after their local wetlands, possibly by not draining the land or by using fewer chemicals. The second way is to make them nature reserves, so that no agriculture or industry can take place around them. But turning a wetland into a reserve means more than just putting up fences and leaving it alone. Even when a wetland site is protected it can still be at risk from pollution from nearby rivers or other, unprotected, wetlands.

New wetlands

Another way to make up for the damage done to wetland habitats is to create new ones. There is a long tradition of artificial wetlands, including rice paddies and the Norfolk Broads in eastern England. The Broads formed when floodwaters filled up holes left by medieval peat diggers.

Brand new wetlands

Today, engineers can create new wetlands by flooding abandoned quarries, gravel pits and mines. To encourage plants and wildlife, it is best to design these wetlands with shallow bays and irregular edges.

Farmers also create new wetlands between their fields and rivers or established wetland sites. These new habitats act as "buffer zones". This means they absorb fertilizers or farm slurry and prevent toxic chemicals from getting into the water system. While they are not suitable places for most species, these new wetlands can support reeds – which work to filter out pollutants – and certain plants that thrive in the sort of nutrient-rich waters that fertilizers produce.

New from old

Ecologists can also turn existing watery places, such as abandoned reservoirs and

Part of the London Wetland Centre in Barnes, London: a new habitat created from disused Victorian reservoirs.

neglected ponds, into new wetland habitats. The London Wetland Centre is on the site of four disused Victorian reservoirs. It has become a home for around 300,000 wetland plants, 140 bird species and 18 types of dragonflies and damselflies.

WETLAND HOMELAND

Old wetlands that have dried up can be restored. For 5,000 years, an Arab people, the Ma'dan, or Marsh Arabs, who are descended from the ancient Sumerian civilization, lived in the wetlands of southern Iraq. In the 1990s, they opposed Iraq's president, Saddam Hussein. In punishment, he diverted the rivers that fed the marshes. As a result the wetlands dried out and the Marsh Arabs became homeless. Today, after the fall of Saddam Hussein's government, scientists are helping the Marsh Arabs re-divert the rivers to their wetlands, bringing back water to about 40% of the region. By the middle of 2004 it was thought that up to 40,000 Marsh Arabs had returned to their ancient homeland.

A Marsh Arab woman and an Oxfam engineer discuss plans to restore wetland habitats in southern Iraq.

Changing attitudes

In the past 50 years, attitudes to wetlands have changed a lot. We have learnt to value these precious habitats more and more, both as homes for plants and animals and as places that benefit human communities. Environmental campaigners hope that this change in attitudes will spread wider still, until the world's wetlands are no longer at risk.

Old views

Many people used to regard wetlands as dangerous, mysterious, disease-ridden places that stood in the way of farmers having dry land for grazing animals and planting crops, and prevented developers from building roads, factories and houses. The result of this attitude was large-scale draining. In the United States, for example, between the 18th and 20th centuries, people drained around 54% of the nation's wetlands. Since the mid-19th century, around 90% of New Zealand's wetlands have disappeared.

The value of wetlands

Today, far fewer people hold these attitudes. However, educating people about the value of wetlands is still very important. Organizations such as the World Wide Fund for Nature (WWF) believe that it is particularly important to educate politicians and business people, who usually make the decisions that can affect a wetland's future.

One way to attract the attention of the individuals who make such decisions is to point out the money wetlands can save governments and businesses by providing such services as flood control and water storage. In 2004, the WWF estimated that the economic value of wetlands was around $70 billion per year.

This peaceful scene in a European river valley demonstrates that farming can go hand-in-hand with successful wetlands management.

ARAL SEA WARNING

The Aral Sea provides a grim lesson of what can happen if people do not protect wetlands. The sea, which borders the countries of Kazakhstan and Uzbekistan in Central Asia, used to be the fourth-largest lake in the world. The estuaries of two rivers that entered the sea also formed major wetland habitats on its shores. But in the 1960s engineers built canals to take water from the rivers to irrigate farmland hundreds of miles away. The canals reduced the amount of water that flowed into the sea. This same water had also maintained the wetlands. Today, the volume of water in the sea is about 75% lower than it was in 1960. People as well as wildlife have suffered from the loss of water. One problem is the dry dust that lies on the exposed sea beds. Local people who breathe this dust, which contains salt, fertilizers and old chemicals, can suffer from a range of health problems. International organizations such as the United Nations and the World Bank are trying to save the Aral Sea and improve the region's environment, but scientists warn that all the waters could disappear by around 2025, leaving nothing but a large, dusty desert.

The Aral Sea has shrunk to about one-quarter of its original size. This has destroyed huge wetland areas.

What can you do?

Here are some suggestions for you to help save and encourage wetland habitats.

Create a wetland!

Make your own pond at school or in your local area. The following tips will help you:

Your pond will need to be at least 60 cm (24 in) deep so that animals can escape ice in winter and hot water in summer.

You will need shallow edges around your pond for animals to get in and out of the water.

You will need to line your pond so the water does not leak out. Most garden centres sell pond liners.

You will need to include pond plants that provide the water with oxygen. Examples of these types of plants include milfoil and water starwort. Try to create marshy areas around the pond by planting species such as marsh marigold.

Remember to get the permission and help of an adult before you start.

Shop carefully

When you and your family go shopping, remember that the products you buy can make a difference to the environment. Don't buy garden products containing peat. Good substitutes include manure or chopped bark. Alternatively, you could try making your own compost.

Consider buying environmentally-friendly washing-up liquids and washing powders. The detergent in them breaks down quite easily, and is less harmful to plants and animals.

Consider buying organic food, which farmers produce without using as many fertilizers or pesticides. Organic food is often more expensive, but the more people buy it, the more farmers will grow it and the cheaper it will become.

Conserve water

Try to limit the amount of water you use. Turn off the tap when you brush your teeth and consider having a quick shower instead of a bath. If you need water for a garden, think about using a water barrel to collect rainwater, which you can then use to water plants.

You could also carry out a water survey in your school or home. Make a list of all the things that use running water, such as taps, toilets and showers. Check that there is no water leaking from any of them. Now think if there are any ways you can save water. Could you, for example, use a water barrel for watering a garden? Or a water-saving shower head in the bathroom?

Find out more

The following websites will give you more information about threatened wetlands aound the world, how people are trying to save them and what you can do to help.

www.panda.org
This is the website of the World Wide Fund for Nature (WWF). Follow the links to the WWF's Living Waters pages to find out about its work protecting wetland habitats.

www.ramsar.org
The website of the Ramsar Convention on Wetlands of International Importance. Read about the work of Ramsar, as well as how to mark World Wetlands Day, which takes place on February 2nd each year.

www.nps.gov/ever/eco
Learn all about the Florida Everglades. There are profiles of different animals as well as information about how people are restoring the Everglades.

www.nationalgeographic.com/features96/okavango
Take a cyber safari around this amazing African wetland, where you can discover facts about the animals that live there.

www.wwtlearn.org.uk
This website, created by the UK's Wildfowl and Wetlands Trust, includes wetland fact files and interactive games.

www.timeforcitizenship.com/teachers/wetlands.asp
The children of Westfield Park Primary School in the UK produced this website, which contains information about the world's wetlands as well as the school's own wetland.

Glossary

Acidic
The state of something, such as a liquid, that enables it to form an acid. Vinegar is an example of an acidic liquid. Bog water is highly acidic, and only a few types of highly specialized plants can grow in it successfully.

Carbon dioxide
A gas, also called CO_2, that is released when fuel, such as wood and coal, burns. It is also breathed out by animals and absorbed by plants in the process of photosynthesis (making oxygen and food from sunlight, water and CO_2).

Carnivorous
Meat eating. Carnivorous plants do not eat insects in the same way that animals do, but break down their bodies with digestive juices and extract the nutrients.

Ecologist
A scientist who studies the relationship between living things and their habitats.

Erosion
The removal of soils and rocks by the movement of water and wind.

Estuary
The part of a river that flows into the sea.

Fen
Low land that is partly or entirely covered with water unless artificially drained. Fens usually have peaty soil. Sedges and reeds grow on fens.

Fertilizer
A substance that farmers spread on the land to help their soil grow better crops. Fertilizer can be natural (made from manure) or artificial (made from a mixture of chemicals).

Floodplain
Flat land alongside a river or other waterway that becomes flooded when the river bursts it banks. Many of the world's biggest floodplains are seasonal. This means they are submerged during the wet season but are dry enough for grazing animals in the dry season.

Food chain
A natural system in which larger organisms feed off smaller ones. At the top of most food chains are larger mammals or birds; at the bottom are plants.

Gills
The part of a fish's body that allows it to breathe. Gills are made up of tiny thread-like filaments, which absorb oxygen from water into a fish's bloodstream.

Global warming
The possible warming of the Earth's temperature, and changes in its weather patterns, because of, scientists believe, too much CO_2 in the atmosphere.

Hydroelectric power
A form of electricity that harnesses the energy of falling or fast-flowing water. Hydroelectric power stations are often built underneath dams. Water comes from the dam down pipes; it then drives turbines, which convert the water's energy into electricity.

Irrigation
An artificial system that channels water through farmland to help farmers grow crops.

Malaria
A disease that mosquitoes carry and spread to humans by biting them. Malaria can damage vital body organs and lead to death if it is not treated. It is a massive killer: around one million babies and children die from the disease each year.

Mangrove
A species of tree that stands high on stilt-, or knee-like roots, and can survive in saltwater swamps.

Marsh
A wetland in which emergent plants, such as reeds, sedges and bulrushes, are the most dominant plant species.

Nomads
People who have no fixed home and move about over a particular region or territory.

Nutrients
Minerals that plants take from the soil to help them grow.

Peatland
A wetland in which peat builds up. Plants living on the surface of a bog, such as sphagnum mosses, bog cotton and heather, do not rot when they die because the ground is waterlogged. Instead they form peat. Bogs, fens and tundra are all types of peatland.

The only source of water for bogs is from the rain, while fens also get water from rivers or underground springs and so contain more nutrients and can support more life. Tundra is frozen peatland, but the top layer thaws in the summer months.

Pesticide
A toxic substance that people use to kill unwanted plants or animals, particularly insects.

Salt marsh
A coastal wetland that is home to sea grasses and wading birds.

Sediment
Particles of sand, mud, minerals or waste matter that settle at the bottom of wetlands and rivers.

Swamp
A wetland in which shrubs and trees are the most dominant plant species.

Tidal flat
A flat muddy surface alongside an estuary. Tidal flats are submerged at high tides and exposed at low tides. The mud of tidal flats is usually rich in nutrients and supports animals such as crabs and worms.

United Nations
A council of nations formed after the Second World War (1939–45) to promote international stability and co-operation.

Index